TONY STEWART

2005 Nextel Cup Champion

David Poole

Peter L. Bannon publisher

Joseph J. Bannon Sr. publisher

Susan M. Moyer senior managing editor

Lynnette A. Bogard acquisitions and developmental editor

K. Jeffrey Higgerson art director

Kenneth J. O'Brien cover and interior design, imaging

Heidi Norsen and Dustin J. Hubbart imaging

Erin Linden-Levy photo editor

ISBN: 1-59670-053-X
© 2005 by David Poole

Front and back cover photos by Worth Canoy/Icon SMI

Printed in the United States of America

Sports Publishing L.L.C.
804 North Neil Street • Champaign, IL 61820
Phone: 1-877-424-2665 • Fax: 217-363-2073
www.SportsPublishingLLC.com

(photo by: Worth Canoy/Icon SMI)

(photo by: Worth Canoy/Icon SMI)

Contents

(photo by: Jerome Davis/Icon SMI)

CHAPTER 1

A few days before the greatest day of his life, Tony Stewart ate a salad at the Dairy Queen in his hometown of Columbus, Ind.

"Usually when he comes in he gets a chili dog or, if he's trying to eat right, a chicken sandwich on a wheat bun," said Bob Franke, the owner of the store at Third and Lafayette streets in the town of 40,000 that has become both Stewart's refuge and his rejuvenation.

"I said, 'If you're going to be climbing fences after winning races, you need to eat more salads,'" said Franke, who was one of the first people to ever believe in the man who now, after winning the 2005 championship, is a two-time NASCAR champion.

"So he ate a salad," Franke said. "But he still had his chocolate milk shake."

Ah, those chocolate shakes. They were part of the deal between Franke and a 10-year-old Tony Stewart. Franke would sponsor the go-karts that Stewart was racing at the local fairgrounds. In return, Stewart and his family would tell the other racers and their families that the DQ would be a good place for them to grab a bite on their way home after races.

And Tony got free milk shakes.

"It all kind of grew out of that," Franke said. "And one thing that's important is that Tony's loyalty from that time to where he is today has never faltered."

In the nearly 25 years that Stewart has been drinking Bob Franke's free milk shakes, he's grown from a 10-year-old boy whose father drove him to focus on being the best he could be into a 34-year-old racer who is, by virtual acclamation,

The 2005 NASCAR Nextel Cup season would see a more relaxed, yet equally determined Tony Stewart. *(photo by: David Griffin/Icon SMI)*

regarded as the most versatile superstar in the world of motorsports today.

He added to his already glittering resume in spectacular fashion in the 2005 NASCAR Nextel Cup season, winning his second championship in four years behind a stunning midseason streak of five race victories in a seven-race stretch that took him to the top of the standings—as well as to the tops of a couple of fences he climbed in celebration.

Stewart dazzled the stock-car racing world with a consistent, strong march through the rest of NASCAR's "regular season" that sent him into the 10-race Chase for the NASCAR Nextel Cup with the lead and momentum that helped carry him through a tight fight to the finish with Jimmie Johnson and emerging star Carl Edwards.

Despite his immense talent and remarkable competitive drive, however, things have rarely come easy to Tony Stewart.

Sure, he became the first driver to ever sweep the U.S. Auto Club championships in the Sprint, Midget and Silver Crown series.

But on his way to winning that "triple crown" in 1995, Stewart had to endure his share of tough times, including strains that racing put on his parents' marriage

and Stewart's relationship with them. Stewart lived with other families and drove wreckers or worked other jobs because he wasn't sure if he'd ever have the money to make a living on the track.

Stewart then became champion of the Indy Racing League, a series that seemed to be tailor-made to fit his life's story with its initial goal to give American drivers the opportunity to excel in open-wheel, oval track racing.

But as he won the 1997 championship in the IRL, Stewart's internal fire sometimes burned out of control. His nickname went from "Tony the Tiger" to "Tony the Temper," and his frustration with being unable to win a race at the one track where it would mean the most brought particular anguish.

Stewart defended that IRL title in 1998, but he also drove in the NASCAR Busch Series for Joe Gibbs Racing. And though he failed to win a race that season, he showed anyone who was watching that the talent he'd shown in a sprint car and in an Indy car could also transfer to a stock car.

So when he won three races and finished fourth in the final points standings as a rookie in NASCAR's top series the following year, nobody was really all that surprised. Stewart's

For the second year in a row, Jimmie Johnson (left) would figure heavily into the Nextel Chase for the Championship. *(photo by: Brian Cleary/Icon SMI)*

abilities in a race car are undeniable, no matter what the car is.

He won a Cup-circuit-best six races the following year as teammate Bobby Labonte won Joe Gibbs Racing its first NASCAR championship. Stewart won three more times in 2001 and finished second in the standings to Jeff Gordon.

And then, in 2002, he added three more race victories and a championship. Statistically, at least, he was on top of America's racing world. But the success had come with a heavy price.

Even during that championship season—in fact, especially during it—Stewart began to chafe against the reins his celebrity as one of the top stars in

America's most popular racing series were placing on him.

When he'd go to a dirt track somewhere to see one of the sprint car teams he'd started compete and just to hang out with the guys who he just loved being around, it wasn't the same. Someone always wanted him to sign an autograph or pose for a picture, and that's exactly what he was trying to get away from.

Although he had bought the house he grew up in back in Columbus when it came on the market, he was living in North Carolina. Joe Gibbs Racing, like most major NASCAR Nextel Cup teams, is based in the Charlotte area, and that's where Stewart thought he needed to be.

The offices for Indianapolis Motor Speedway sit on the corner of 16th Street and Georgetown. Many youngsters from Indiana have dreamed of racing at the track's hallowed grounds. *(photo by: Kevin Reece/Icon SMI)*

2005 Nextel Cup Champion

2005 started off in typical fashion for the No. 20 team...slowly.
(photo by: Jim Redman/Icon SMI)

But the more time he spent there, the more it felt to Stewart like he was always at work. Racers are celebrities in the Charlotte area, and when Stewart ventured out into public the people who saw him wanted to see Tony Stewart, the race car driver. Stewart didn't want to be that guy all of the time, but for a long and sometimes painful period he wasn't completely aware of the toll those demands were taking on him.

It has always been part of Stewart's makeup to despise losing. That's a big part of the reason, in fact, he's so good at what he does. Over the early years of his career, that trait sometimes manifested itself in ways that only added to the pressures that were building on him.

Once after a race at Richmond he was chastised by NASCAR for driving too fast as he went to the garage crowded with crews, media and fans in the immediate aftermath of the checkered flag. After a penalty from NASCAR he didn't agree with at Daytona, he argued with a NASCAR official and knocked a tape recorder from a reporter's hands.

There were times, times when Stewart thought it was right to be dealing with fans, when he could be totally charming. But when someone asked for an autograph at a moment Stewart felt inappropriate, he often did not react well. In interviews, he could be thoughtful and incisive. Or, depending on his mood, he could be short and insulting.

Finally, and in terms of where it happened, predictably, the nadir came at Indianapolis Motor Speedway in August 2002.

Stewart spent most of his adolescent years dreaming of racing at the historic Indianapolis track. To this day, he talks about driving a wrecker along Georgetown Road, which runs directly parallel to the frontstretch, allowing

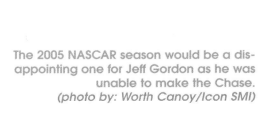

The 2005 NASCAR season would be a disappointing one for Jeff Gordon as he was unable to make the Chase.
(photo by: Worth Canoy/Icon SMI)

2005 Nextel Cup Champion

himself to imagine what it would be like to be just on the other side of that fence.

And when the got to the Indy Racing League, part of the dream came true. Stewart raced in the Indianapolis 500. What's more, he knew that there were years when he had the fastest car at Indy in the month of May. The opportunity to win at the Brickyard was right there, but he never had been able to grasp it completely. It seemed the harder he tried, the harder his heart was broken.

On August 4, 2002, Stewart led 43 laps in the NASCAR Brickyard 400 at Indy. His No. 20 Home Depot-sponsored Pontiac was strong—strong enough to win, no question about it—like some of his Indy cars had been there. But late in the race, Stewart lost the handling and NASCAR veteran Bill Elliott won instead.

Stewart faded badly in the waning laps and finished 12th. Immediately after the checkered flag, he drove into the garage and parked his car near the garage stall where the team had worked on it. He got out and immediately started walking toward the team's transporter. A photographer, doing free lance work for the *Indianapolis Star*, started walking along with Stewart taking pictures.

Stewart's anger had finally reached a point where it had to go somewhere, and that photographer wound up being

where it went. Stewart shoved at him as they walked, and several people saw what happened. A firestorm of controversy as heated as the anger Stewart let out that day followed.

Stewart was fined by his sponsor and sanctioned by NASCAR. Fans booed him and members of his own team barely managed to hold in their own frustrations over their driver's actions.

Stewart was more than 200 points out of first in the NASCAR Cup standings after that. But somehow, he and his team pulled together the very next weekend at Watkins Glen, N.Y., and Stewart won the race. Over the final months of that season, Stewart finished in the top 10 in 10 of the final 15 races. When he finished 18th in the season's finale at Homestead, Fla., it was enough for him to hold off Mark Martin by 38 points to win the championship.

That title, however, did not heal all of the wounds.

He won two races in 2003 and two more in 2004, but finished outside the top five in the final standings in both of those seasons.

Off the track, Stewart continued to struggle to find a balance in his life, an equilibrium that would allow him to compete and do what he loves to do—race—while still finding a way within all of the demands that come with being a NASCAR star to simply be the same Tony Stewart who liked going down to the Dairy Queen in Columbus to get his free milk shakes.

To find himself, he wound up going right back to where it all started.

While professionally 2002 was the pinnacle of Stewart's distinguished career, personally it was a painful and difficult year for him. (photo by: Brian Cleary/Icon SMI)

(photo by: John Pyle/Icon SMI)

TONY

CHAPTER 2

The best way to Tony Stewart's house from downtown Columbus includes a turn onto Home Avenue. Nothing could be more appropriate.

Stewart never hated the Charlotte area, specifically. He'd moved there after beginning his NASCAR Nextel Cup career because that's where his team was and that's where most of the other drivers lived. He had a nice house—a very nice house—and shared it with friends who were members of his and other crews in the sport. They hung out and had a good time together.

One of those friends, however, accompanied Stewart on a trip back to Columbus for a visit late in the 2004 racing season.

"When we got back to Charlotte he said I was a totally different person when I got on that plane and when I got off that plane," Stewart said. "That wasn't something I'd really thought of, and it did change my attitude about living in the Charlotte area compared to living in Indiana.

"It wasn't that I didn't like the Charlotte area. It's awesome. There are probably five times more things to do in Charlotte than where I live. But there's just something about living in your hometown and something about being around the same friends you ran around with when you raced go-karts or three-quarter midgets or sprint cars or something like that. It's just a different atmosphere."

During 2004, another major decision helped Stewart think more seriously about spending more of his time in Indiana. He purchased the legendary Eldora Speedway, a dirt track in

The two places that Tony Stewart feels most at home are in a race car and in his home-town of Columbus, Ind. *(photo by: Worth Canoy/Icon SMI)*

Rossburg, Ind., about an hour's drive from Indianapolis that's one of the most beloved tracks in the racing-crazed Midwest. Although Stewart has plenty of people to run that track on a weekly basis, being its owner only deepened his sense of roots in the area where he grew up.

Columbus is a typical small town in many ways, but the hometown of the 1950s singing group the Four Freshmen and of Chuck Taylor, who developed the high-top basketball sneaker that helped make Converse famous, does have one very unique distinction.

In 1942, a charitable foundation set up by Cummins Engine Company, which has for more than 75 years made small diesel engines and is still the city's largest employer, paid architect Eliel Saarinen's fee for designing a new building for the town's First Christian Church. In the

Tony and Zippy may not share the same parents or heritage, but they do share the same passion and desire for racing. *(photo by: Erik Perel/Icon SMI)*

years since, world-renowned architects like I.M. Pei and Richard Meier have been commissioned to design nearly 60 public buildings, schools and churches. As a result, Columbus now ranks sixth on the American Institute of Architects list for architectural innovation and design—behind Chicago, New York City, San Francisco, Boston, and Washington, D.C.

As of a few days after the end of the 2004 racing season, Columbus also once again had the distinction of having one of America's best race car drivers among its nearly 40,000 residents.

The home in which Stewart grew up is not a mansion, by any definition of that term. It is a lovely but modest house in a lovely, middle-class neighborhood with large yards for children to play in. Many of the people who live there now lived there back when Stewart was doing exactly that.

"The neighbors in front of me and behind me and on both sides of me—you go one direction beside me and three houses down, they're all the same," Stewart says. "That's part of what helps keep me grounded and maintain the sanity I guess, from a certain standpoint of not being bombarded with people that live next door and want to snoop and see what you're doing. These people don't care. They've seen me since I was a little

kid. I'm the same kid that used to play baseball in the back yard and smack a baseball into the aluminum siding of their house and they'd come out screaming.

"They're used to having me around. They're happy I'm back. Also, a cool side of it, is when I'm gone they're watching that house like a hawk because they know how much it means to me. We make sure that if the neighbors need something if something happens or if they need us to take care of a dog when we're home, they know we'll do it for them. We have keys to their houses if they need something. ...I feel very comfortable every time I go home."

Stewart's attitude going into the 2005 Nextel Cup season also underwent a significant adjustment following a meeting with his team during the final weeks of 2004.

"That's the best thing that happened," Stewart said of the meeting. "I sat down with my race team and let them vent for a day and it was one of the most productive meetings as a race team that we've had since I've been there. We got a lot of things out in the air."

Greg Zipadelli, who has been Stewart's crew chief ever since they came into the sport together in 1999, called that meeting.

Tony takes in the warm Daytona Beach sun as he begins his seventh run for the NASCAR Cup. *(photo by: Brian Cleary/Icon SMI)*

"I get to listen and see both sides," Zipadelli said, "from Tony to my guys and their morale and things like that.

"I called Tony down from Indy to sit with the guys so they could talk to him. They just basically explained to him on how some of the things he did and the ways that he acted affected their lives. If you don't stop to think about it sometimes, it's hard to understand how every truck driver going down the road is affected by something you did at the race track.

"But we're a family and I think those guys have to share some of that stuff with him that they've experienced. That kind of opened his eyes to how big this family is and what they go through when he has a bad day."

"Tony is a big part of this team. A lot of his attitude and the way he shows up, like myself, if I show up and I'm in a bad mood and I'm taking it out on the guys, then you've kind of set the tone for the weekend. We have a lot of responsibilities but I think one of them is being the best leaders we can. Be their friends, be people. It's important that Tony and myself set that tone. You ask a lot of those

(photo by: Worth Canoy/Icon SMI)

guys, and we need to give that back to them."

Stewart has nothing but praise for Zipadelli's role in the team's success.

"We have the same passion and desire to win," Stewart said. "He understands me and I understand him. I've never been married but I feel that with some of my buddies it's almost like we are married. When I'm having a bad day he has ways to pick me up and when he's having a bad day I have ways to pick him up.

"We're like brothers, basically. We'll be out and people will ask us if we're brothers. I don't know if my milkman was Italian or my mailman was Italian but I know my father wasn't Italian. It's fun to watch people around us thinking we're related."

Tony attributes the success and longevity of their relationship (they have been together longer than any other active crew chief/driver combination in the sport) to Zippy's patience and tolerance.

"He's (Zipadelli) a very tolerant and patient person, I know that. To work with me you have to be. But I think first and foremost we realized from day one that we both had the same passion and

Tony Stewart leads Kurt Busch enroute to victory in the Dodge Savemart 350 at Infineon Raceway. It was the first of five trips to Victory Lane for the No. 20 team.
(photo by: Brian Cleary/Icon SMI)

desire to win races. When you get two people with the same desire and the same passion, you always find a way of working well together.

"I think there have been times where he's wanted to knock my head off. But every time that's come around he's had a legitimate reason for that. But I think it shows how strong a person Zippy really is. He's never given up on me. There's been a bunch of times where he has been really frustrated and disappointed with me, but he has never turned his back on me. No matter how good or bad our career goes from here on out, he's the guy I want to do it with."

Stewart and Zipadelli got 2005 off to a good start at Daytona. He won his 125-mile qualifying race and, after making a remarkable save by driving through the grass and back up onto the track going into Turn 1, won the Busch Series race the day before the Daytona 500.

In the 500, Stewart started fourth and led 107 of 203 laps. But he couldn't make that strong pay off with a victory and he wound up finishing seventh.

In the final laps, Jimmie Johnson and Stewart made contact with each other as

Stewart and Johnson would have their share of run-ins over the course of the 2005 season, however, Stewart would eventually come out on top.
(photo by: Erik Perel/Icon SMI)

they raced for position. Stewart gave Johnson a little retaliatory tap on the cool-down lap, earning him and Johnson a postrace visit to the NASCAR hauler.

"We were trading cooking secrets," Stewart joked. "It was fine. We're racing and it's the last lap of the Daytona 500. I was mad he pinched me into the No.10 (Scott Riggs). We went down there and we both bumped into each other. We both did the same thing to each other. So, you know, it's fine. We both had good weeks here, we both finished in the top 10. He finished fifth and I finished seventh. We're both leaving here in a good situation in points."

It would not be the last time they'd see each other in 2005.

Tony Stewart (20) spins in turn four as Elliott Sadler (38) and Brian Vickers (25) drive past during the Food City 500 NASCAR Nextel Cup series race at Bristol Motor Speedway in Bristol, TN.
(photo by: Erik Perel/Icon SMI)

Tony Stewart wins the second Gatorade Duel at Daytona NASCAR Nextel Cup series race at Daytona International Speedway in Daytona Beach, FL.

(photo by: Erik Perel/Icon SMI)

CHAPTER 3

Tony Stewart left Daytona in February 2005 with a seventh-place finish and 156 points in the first of 36 races that would determine the year's NASCAR Nextel Cup champion.

He'd led more that half of the laps run in the series biggest race, 107 of 203 run in a race that featured a green-white-checkered finish and a Jeff Gordon victory, and despite the fact that he lost some ground late in the race his season's start was a lot better than it had been in 2002, when he won his first career Cup title.

In the 2002 Daytona 500, Stewart completed just two laps before he lost an engine in the No. 20 Chevrolet. He finished 43rd—last—in that race and started the year out as far behind as he possibly could have before rallying for the title.

But in 2005, Stewart didn't lead another lap after Daytona until the season's sixth race at Martinsville. He led 247 laps in that race, again the most of anybody, but lug nuts left loose on a pit stop caused his right-front wheel to wobble and, on lap 432 in a 500-lap race, fall off the car.

Stewart finished 26th at Martinsville. The next week at Texas, a crankshaft broke and there was a subsequent fire under the car that left Stewart with some painful burns on his thighs and right elbow. He finished 31st there. At Phoenix, he got involved in another bumping incident with Jimmie Johnson and finished 33rd.

Eight races into the season, Stewart was 14th in the standings and looking for something to turn things around.

Stewart won the NASCAR Busch series race in February at Daytona and led the most laps in the Cup race. However, Jeff Gordon would go on to win his fourth Daytona 500. *(photo by: Kevin Thorne/Icon SMI)*

"We're just having a period where we're struggling," he said. "It has just been a little bit of everything. We've been off on our aero program some. ...I'm not sure what the problem is, but hopefully we'll find it soon to where we can get the issues addressed. The main thing is to get ourselves back in the top 10 in points and be in a position to compete when those last 10 races start, hopefully we'll have all the issues solved by then."

It has not been unusual for Stewart and his team to start slow in NASCAR Nextel Cup seasons. As a rookie, it took until Richmond in September for him to get his first win. There was also the last-place finish to open what turned out to be a title season in 2002.

"It just seems historically that we normally have a slow start when the tracks are cooler, and it seems like the tracks have a lot more grip that way," Stewart said. "It seems like when we get into May, June, and July that we really hit our stride, when the tracks are starting to get warmer and slicker it's getting harder to get grip on the race track. That seems like to the point where we really start gaining momentum.

Tony Stewart (20) and Dale Earnhardt Jr (8) race along the front stretch of Daytona International Speedway during the 2005 Daytona 500.
(photo by: David Griffin/Icon SMI)

A test at Michigan International Speedway would prove pivotal in the 2005 season for the No. 20 team. *(photo by: Brian Cleary/Icon SMI)*

"So I always look forward to the month of May coming around. But I don't feel a sense of urgency of trying to get back on track. I feel like we're just kind of in a learning process. We're not really on par like we've been in the past, but I'm not feeling like we'd better find this soon or we're going to be in big trouble.

"It's just a matter of doing what we've been doing and keeping the guys pumped up on the race team. Sooner or later we're going to find something. With this caliber of a race team, you don't win a championship by not knowing what you're supposed to do. It's just a matter of saying there's a missing piece of the equation and this team is capable of finding it. I think we'll be fine."

As the warmth of spring spread across the NASCAR racing world, there were some signs of life from the No. 20 team. Stewart finished second at Talladega and 10th at Charlotte to move back into the top 10 in the standings, and then at Richmond he chased Kasey Kahne much of the evening and finished second as Kahne, whose background in U.S. Auto Club competition is strikingly similar to Stewart's, got his first career NASCAR Nextel Cup victory.

But almost as quickly as they'd headed in the right direction, things skated off course again for the team at Charlotte, where Stewart finished 24th; at Dover, where he ran 15th, and at Pocono, where the No. 20 wound up 29th. Stewart didn't lead a lap in any of those races and he also failed to finish on the lead lap in all three.

Going into the season's first race at Michigan International Speedway on June 19, Stewart was 10th in the points. It really didn't matter a whole lot that he was 380 points behind leader Jimmie Johnson, since under the Chase for the NASCAR Nextel Cup format that was in its second year he only needed to be in the top 10 after 26 races to make the 10-race championship "playoff." But what did matter was that just past the halfway mark in the 26-race run to the Chase, Stewart was in the thick of a pack that had 15 drivers within 223 points of one another vying for spots three through 10 in the standings.

The season was at a crossroads. Three good weeks followed by three mediocre ones wasn't going to cut it.

NASCAR is different from other professional sports in many ways, but one way in which it's very similar is that success often stems from the hard work that gets done when the spotlight isn't on. Training camps, two-a-day practices, hours of working on the fundamentals are all part of what makes football, basketball and baseball teams stand out. In racing, it's the work done by the dozens of people who work long hours at the shop, seeking a few tenths of a second here and there. And it's also what gets done on those days the driver and crew spend at the race track testing, making lap after lap when the grandstands are empty and there's no checkered flag—at least on that day—to race toward.

And it is no exaggeration whatsoever to say that Stewart's path to the 2005 NASCAR Nextel Cup championship began on a day just like that at Michigan in early June. Even as the team was struggling to get good finishes on race day—or, perhaps, precisely because of that—they were working to find those tiny pieces of the puzzle that seemed to be missing.

Tony Stewart answers questions from the media regarding his team's chances for the 2005 season. *(photo by: David Griffin/Icon SMI)*

2005 Nextel Cup Champion

After the race at Michigan International Speedway in June, Tony Stewart fans had a lot to look forward to and cheer about. *(photo by: Brian Cleary/Icon SMI)*

Stewart and Zipadelli came away from the Michigan test encouraged. They felt they'd found something that would help them keep up with Johnson, who'd posted two wins and 11 top-10 finishes in the first 14 races to grab the points lead. They were also chasing Greg Biffle, who'd started the season in a blaze—especially at the 1.5- and 2-mile intermediate tracks where the No. 20 team had been searching for speed.

Stewart was pleased when his car was fast in practice and when he qualified third for the Batman Begins 400 at the 2-mile Michigan track. He led 97 laps in the race and seemed to be in good shape to get his first win of the season.

But when Sterling Marlin blew an engine late in the race, Zipadelli brought Stewart to pit road for four fresh tires. Several cars, including Biffle's, stayed on the track and a few others changed only two tires. Stewart was eighth for the restart with 27 laps to go, but with four new tires and a strong Chevrolet he figured that'd be more than enough time for him to get the lead back.

Instead it was Biffle who, even on old tires, parlayed track position into his fifth victory of the year. Stewart finished

Teamwork has been the key to success for the No. 20 team in 2005.
(photo by: Brian Cleary/Icon SMI)

2005 Nextel Cup Champion

second, but afterward his frustration was difficult to mask.

"I think we found some things that made us faster here," he said of the test that had set up the good run. "Whether it is anything we can take away from here and take somewhere else, I don't know. ...But you know it's like, what are we missing now? We made a huge step and we're still not where we need to be. It's like, what do we need to do to catch those guys.

"I guess we need to figure out how to lead the right lap. It's frustrating for us as a team. We had a really good car all day (but) what do we have to do to get in victory lane this season?

"It's like Zippy said, we got to crawl before we walk, walk before we jog and jog before we run. So, you know, I'm sure in 10 minutes I'll feel a lot better about it, it's just that when you run that good all day and lead that many laps and you can't finish it off...All I knew is that we weren't fast enough to beat Biffle."

What Stewart could not have known on that afternoon as he sat in an interview room and lamented his inability to finish off the strong run at Michigan with his 20th career win was just how significant that day would turn out to be for him.

But even though the season to that point had been challenging, there had already been some things going on with the team that were very different from years past. The effects of the late-season meeting from the year before and Stewart's new-found peace afforded by his return to live in the home he grew up in were coming together to change the whole environment on the No. 20 team.

"From the start of the season we've had fun racing as a team," Stewart said. "Even the days where we've had problems, that has made it easier to go back to the shop and stick together as a team and not get down.

"When you have a team effort like that and a support group like that, if one person gets down it's easy to have that many guys that are on your side to help pick you up. We just have fun. We've simplified it. This series is so complicated with media and sponsor commitments and commitments with the race team. It's hard to have a life, so it's hard to keep a positive attitude.

"We find more things to do as a team now than we've ever done before. Whether it's playing cards or going to watch a movie or whatever it is. We've done it together and we're having fun, even though the results haven't shown this year. This is probably one of the

2005 Nextel Cup Champion

(photo by: Brian Cleary/Icon SMI)

worst seasons we've had up until this point. But, at the same time, the attitude of the team is better than it's been since 1999. Even though it isn't the season that we've wanted, it's made it more acceptable. That doesn't mean we're being complacent, but we're all on the same page and we're all working toward the same goal. We're all there to pick each other up and we're having fun with it."

In a weekend that would see Carl Edwards win both the Busch and Cup races and Jimmie Johnson would take over the points lead, Tony Stewart had a disappointing 17th place finish.
(photo by: Craig Peterson/Icon SMI)

2005 Nextel Cup Champion

(photo by: Brian Cleary/Icon SMI)

CHAPTER 4

After the runner-up finish at Michigan, Stewart's third second-place finish of the year, the next race was the Dodge Save/Mart 350 at Infineon Raceway, the road course in Sonoma, Calif. On the Thursday of that week, Stewart appeared at a news conference aimed at Bay Area writers and broadcasters preparing to cover the race and turned the hour-long session into a virtual comedy routine.

After leaving the restaurant where that news conference was held, Stewart took some time to look around in some of the shops in San Francisco's Fisherman's Wharf area. In one of those shops, he saw and bought a flag that he took with him to the track the next day.

"It says, 'The beatings will continue until morale improves,'" Stewart said. "Everybody who has come into our trailer and seen that has laughed. That's just the kind of thing we're doing. Having fun. Picking on each other."

The best way for a NASCAR Nextel Cup team to have fun, however, is for it to win races. Stewart had come close, finishing second at Talladega, Richmond and Michigan and also leading the most laps at Daytona and Martinsville.

The loss to Biffle at Michigan had been particularly galling, since Stewart had fresher tires and still couldn't catch the No. 16 Ford in the waning laps. Even Zipadelli began to wonder what was going on.

"It kind of felt like forever," he said. "I started to doubt myself if we could do it. We've had some good opportunities and we let them slip away. I think Michigan was a big charge for everybody. We were close again and didn't capitalize on it."

The road course at Infineon Raceway, however, provided an opportunity for Stewart and Zipadelli. In his first 12 Cup races on road courses, Stewart had won three times and finished in the top 10 seven times. That kind of record allowed

After being "the first loser" three times in 2005, Stewart was finally able to win one at Sonoma, Calif. *(photo: Brian Cleary/Icon SMI)*

the team to go to the June 26th race with a full measure of confidence.

He qualified seventh, which put him three rows behind pole-winner Jeff Gordon at the green flag. Gordon has eight career road-course wins in Cup competition, and Stewart enjoys measuring himself against that kind of standard when he races. But after leading the first 32 laps, Gordon started having transmission troubles and was never again a factor in the Dodge/Save Mart 350.

It was, instead, Ricky Rudd with whom Stewart would have to deal with to win. Rudd, who has six Cup road-course wins on his resume, took the lead by passing Rusty Wallace on lap 82 in the 110-lap race. But Rudd knew he was about to get some company at the front of the field.

Stewart had been 14th for a restart on lap 73 after pitting under yellow, but he quickly moved back into position to challenge. He passed Wallace on lap 88 to

Tony leads the rest of the field through the "esses" at Infineon Raceway to his first trip to victory lane in 2005. *(photo by: Erik Perel/Icon SMI)*

2005 Nextel Cup Champion

With a win under his belt for the 2005 season, the momentum for the No. 20 team was now heading in the right direction. *(photo by: Craig Peterson/Icon SMI)*

take second and Rudd knew he was in trouble. "I tried to hold him off, but it was just a matter of time," Rudd said. "You can only run over your head for so many laps."

Stewart, however, was dealing with his own issues. He'd lost fourth gear and had his Home Depot Chevy jump out of third gear on him a couple of times. "I could survive without fourth but not without third," Stewart said. "So I just kept holding it in gear and kept trying not to tear it up."

So Stewart had one hand holding his shifter and the other hand on the wheel as he chased down Rudd. He got to the rear bumper of Rudd's No. 21 Ford on lap 95, but Rudd fended off Stewart's first parries in Turn 11, a hairpin near the end of each lap that offers the best opportunity for passing at Infineon Raceway.

"He's smart," Stewart said of Rudd. "I was working pretty hard for a while, trying to make him heat up his tires. But I

Tony Stewart congratulates Kevin Harvick on his victory at Bristol Motor Speedway. Harvick's win would be significant as it was one of the few races won in 2005 by a driver not on either the Hendrick or Roush teams. *(photo by: Worth Canoy/Icon SMI)*

2005 Nextel Cup Champion

Tony Stewart has led a lot of laps at Daytona and Talladega, but the Pepsi 400 at Daytona would bring him his first victory at a restrictor plate race.
(photo by: Brian Cleary/Icon SMI)

Even though the Pepsi 400 at Daytona International Speedway was delayed several hours because of rain, many fans stuck around for the 2 a.m. finish.
(photo by: Worth Canoy/Icon SMI)

was driving one-handed and I started making mistakes. I just took a couple of laps and slowed down and got my rhythm back."

On lap 100, Stewart dug low entering that turn on the 1.99-mile track and got the nose of his car inside of Rudd's. Once he'd powered off the corner with the lead, it was over. He endured one more restart after a late caution, but by that time Rudd was saving fuel so he could hold on for

second. Stewart won by a comfortable 2.26 seconds.

Drivers on the Roush Racing and Hendrick Motorsports teams had won 13 of the season's first 15 races, with only Kahne at Richmond and Kevin Harvick at Bristol breaking that hammerlock.

Now, finally, Stewart was on the board.

"It has been frustrating when you know there are two teams that are really dominant and you have a day where you

Joe Gibbs was on hand to help Tony and team celebrate.
(photo by: Brian Cleary/Icon SMI)

TONY STEWART

Tony Stewart continues his ascent in the NASCAR Nextel Cup Series.
(photo by: Brian Cleary/Icon SMI)

2005 Nextel Cup Champion

feel you've got a chance to win it and you can't capitalize on it," Stewart said of the missed opportunities that had preceded his first 2005 win. "We've had opportunities where we feel we've had a shot at winning the race and something happened where we ended up second or further back. It was just nice to finish one off, period."

On the next weekend, Stewart finished off another one at Daytona. Despite running strong several times,

Stewart had never completed a NASCAR Nextel Cup victory on a restrictor-plate track. But he dominated this Pepsi 400 like nobody ever had, leading an event-record 151 of 160 laps.

Rain held up the start of the race until after 10:30 p.m., but once the green did fly so did Stewart's car. He led the first 103 laps and the nine laps that he didn't lead all night were directly due to pit stops. But, for the third straight week, a decision to take four tires on a late pit

For the second week in a row, Stewart found himself in victory lane.
(photo by: Brian Cleary/Icon SMI)

stop meant Stewart did have to race his way back to the front.

He was fifth on the last restart and immediately lined up behind Matt Kenseth's Ford, giving Kenseth a push down the backstretch that put him alongside Kahne, who'd been the leader on the restart. Kahne had Jimmie Johnson racing behind him. As that front four crossed the start-finish line and roared toward Turn 1 on lap 145, Stewart gathered his own momentum and moved to Kenseth's outside. Johnson, meanwhile, went low of Kahne and, for a few moments, they were four wide.

"When I made my move it was only two-wide," Stewart said. "I made it three-wide. Then the spotter said, 'Four-wide!' But I had a big enough run that it wasn't four-wide for a long time. If we'd gone through Turn 1 four-wide it might have been more of an issue."

After leading the rest of the way, Stewart came around after taking the checkered flag and parked his car under the flag-stand at the start-finish line. Instead of doing a victory burnout, Stewart decided he wanted to celebrate in another way. He climbed the catch fence, gingerly negotiating his way over the part at the top that bends back out over the track. He made it all the way and pumped his fists to a cheering crowd.

"I had to do it once," said Stewart, whose aim was to one-up Indy Car driver Helio Castroneves' "Spiderman" routine. "Nobody ever goes all the way to the top. ...I'm way too old and fat to be doing that

(but) once I started I was committed. Unofficially, I think I am the first guy to go all the way up and over into the flag stand. Helio has come catching up to do."

After winning on a road course and a restrictor-plate track, Stewart had moved all the way up to third in the standings. But he also knew that if he wanted to be a factor in the remaining races before the Chase and in the Chase itself, his cars would have to continue to perform on intermediate tracks the way it had in the run at Michigan.

"That's why I say this weekend is such a pivotal weekend for us," Stewart said before the USG Sheetrock 400 at Chicagoland Speedway. "If we can have a really good weekend, that backs up what we had at Michigan. We had a Michigan test and thought we learned a lot there. Now hopefully what we learned there and what worked for us at Michigan will work for us here. If it doesn't, it tells us we found something that works good at one track. If it works good here, it tells us that we may have found something that's going to help us catch up and close that gap between the Hendrick and Roush teams."

The weekend at Chicagoland got off to a bad start, though, as Stewart cut a tire and crashed his primary car in practice and spent the rest of the day being checked out by doctors. J.J. Yeley qualified the car, and although he was sore from the hard blow he'd taken, Stewart came back the next day to practice his backup car and ran fifth in the race on Sunday after starting from the rear of the field.

Stewart was actually upset after the race that he didn't finish at least second. Pit strategy played a key role in the outcome, with Dale Earnhardt Jr. winning on a fuel-mileage gamble. Matt Kenseth's Ford dominated the race and Stewart felt that, if he'd stayed out to gain track position instead of making a final pit stop, he might have won. But given the circumstances, the fifth-place finish was perfectly acceptable.

"That's what it takes to win championships," Stewart said. "If that happens in the last 10-week stretch and we can pull out a top five in a situation like this, that's what it's going to take. I'm just really proud of everybody.

"This was a very key weekend for us to backup our performance in Michigan. I think we showed that we've caught up with the Roush and Hendrick teams a

J.J. Yeley prepares to qualify the Home Depot No. 20 car of Tony Stewart after Stewart wrecked in practice. *(photo by: Ray Grabowski/Icon SMI)*

little bit. We didn't win the race today. We never led a lap, but we were a contender all day and we were right in that mix with Hendrick and Roush cars. That hopefully will solidify our name at Joe Gibbs Racing in that list of two or three now that have a shot at winning this thing at the end of the year."

The next stop was New Hampshire International Speedway, and Stewart was almost as strong there as he had been at Daytona two weeks earlier. Although Kurt Busch gave him a go over the final 50 laps, Stewart led 232 of 300 circuits of the 1-mile track and won for the third time in four races.

Once again, he celebrated by climbing the fence at the flagstand. This time he got over the fence, then got to the ladder that leads to the stand itself. Once there, he took off his helmet and basked in a crowd reaction that gave him—and just about everyone who witnessed it—goose bumps.

"That was just the coolest thing to see," Stewart said. "As soon as my feet hit the ground they went crazy because they knew what was coming. It didn't matter whether they had Jeff Gordon hats on or Rusty Wallace hats or Dale Jr. hats—they were all cheering. I think they know I'm

Stewart took a hard hit in practice but ended up taking home a fifth place finish in a back-up car at Chicagoland Speedway.
(photo by: Ray Grabowski/Icon SMI)

(photo by: Worth Canoy/Icon SMI)

doing it for them. It didn't matter whether they liked me or hated me, they were still cheering. That was my time to spend with those fans. If every time I get out of the car they get that excited, I don't care how tall that fence is. I'm probably going to fall and bust my butt before it's all over with but I'll keep trying. I'll keep trying to get over the top of them. I'm definitely going to get a trainer, though. That liked to have killed me. I thought I was going to die if I tried to climb down. They said I could go down the steps and through the hole in the fence, and I said, 'Thank you very much.'"

Stewart didn't make it four wins in five races the next week at Pocono Raceway. His seventh-place finish was the first time in six races he'd been out of the top five, but the momentum was still pointing him in the right direction. Going into the final open weekend on the NASCAR 2005 Nextel Cup schedule, Stewart had come from 10th place in the standings, 380 points behind Johnson, all the way to second, just 66 points back.

And it was time to go home.

(photo: Worth Canoy/Icon SMI)

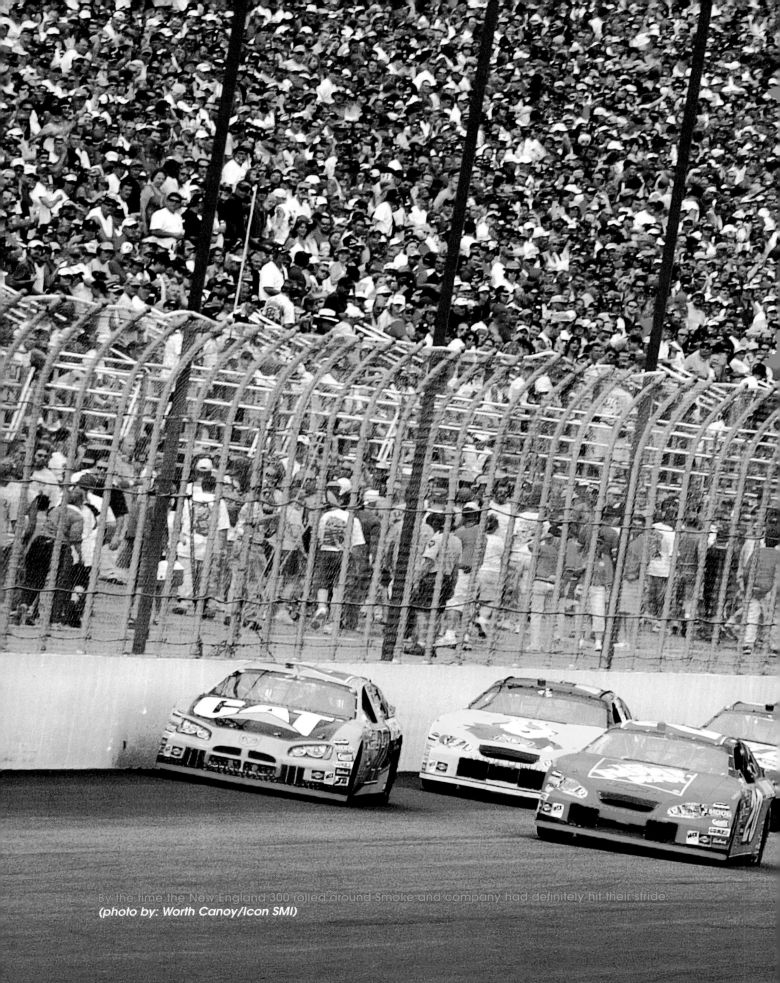

By the time the New England 300 rolled around Smoke and company had definitely hit their stride.
(photo by: Worth Canoy/Icon SMI)

CHAPTER 5

Ernest Wright is 86 years old. He lives close enough to Indianapolis Motor Speedway that he can almost smell the fumes from the cars as they run around the historic 2.5-mile oval.

For several years, on each July 18th, the man everyone calls "Crocky" would go to a grocery store and buy a cake. He'd take it over to the Speedway and share it with the workers there.

Back in 1989, July 18th became an important day on the calendar. He was at a U.S. Auto Club race featuring three-quarter midgets at a track in Madison, Ind., that day, and a young driver named Tony Stewart won the feature.

"I told them," Wright says. "I told everybody before they'd ever heard of him. I knew it as soon as I saw him in practice. I didn't even talk to him that night, but the track wasn't in good shape and everybody was staying down on the

bottom. But Tony was running on the outside."

Dick Jordan, chief of the USAC news bureau, said Wright started talking about Stewart the next day. "Crocky said, 'This guy is coming, get ready,'" Jordan said.

Wright started going to races in 1932 and two years later he started driving midget cars himself. He gave himself 10 years to make it as a driver, but World War II interrupted that and he never got to race at the big track that's across the street from where Wright now lives.

After giving up on a driving career, Wright became a writer. He's written thousands of stories for various publications about USAC events, as well as a four-volume history of midget car racing.

"I've got pictures of three drivers on my wall," Wright said. "Rex Mays, Johnny Thomson and Tony. Rex Mays was my first idol, and I think Johnny Thomson

Back home in Indiana, Stewart would realize a life-long dream.
(photo by: AJ Mast/Icon SMI)

Kasey Kahne and Stewart battled back and forth for the lead at Indianapolis several times before Stewart finally overtook Kahne for good on the last restart.
(photo by: Brian Cleary/Icon SMI)

was the best of all of them. But Tony's up there."

Wright's devotion to USAC racing is evidence of just how important the sport is in the Indianapolis area. Within a 150-mile radius of Indianapolis Motor Speedway, cars sling dirt and burn rubber on pavement at dozens of tracks. Salem, Winchester, Terre Haute and, of course, Eldora—these are places where the true legends of open-wheel racing got their starts and where drivers who never go on to race anywhere else carve out their own places in the region's racing lore.

If open-wheel racing were the Catholic church, then Indianapolis Motor Speedway would be the Vatican. In the same way that every Little League baseball player who's ever stepped up to home plate dreams of one day standing in the batter's box of a Major League Baseball stadium, every young driver who has ever strapped himself into a USAC quarter-midget has thought about what it

(photo by: Streeter Lecka/Getty Images)

The Home Depot Chevrolet races behind Kasey Kahne, driver of the No. 9 Dodge Dealers Dodge, during the NASCAR Nextel Cup Allstate 400 at the Brickyard on August 7, 2005 at Indianapolis Motor Speedway in Indianapolis, Indiana.
(photo by: Streeter Lecka/Getty Images)

would be like to stand in victory lane at The Brickyard.

In his interviews after the victory in the New England 300 at New Hampshire International Speedway, Stewart had made it clear one more time just how much winning at Indy would mean to him.

"If I could give away my championship and just get one win at Indy, I would do it in a heartbeat," he said. "I don't care if I lead one lap at Indy—just as long as it's the right one."

Stewart has never tried to hide his desire to conquer Indianapolis Motor Speedway. "It's just one of those places that consumes you," he said. "It's like Daytona is to all the stock car guys who have grown up around stock car racing all their lives. Indy is just one of those special places. There's no other track like it. There is no other track shaped like it. It's just a neat atmosphere. When you have a track like that with so much history, it's hard not to get consumed in it."

Nelson Stewart, Tony's father, saw what racing at Indy did to his son. "I think the pressure just triples when he comes to Indy," Nelson said. "A lot of his fans are from this area and they want him to win, almost expect him to win. He knows that, and he wants to win, too. He wants to win it for the fans and for himself, and when you start adding all of that up it puts a lot of pressure on him."

Stewart's passion for winning at Indy had become such a regular part of the story whenever he raced at Indy that it

Tony Stewart leads Kasey Kahne across the finish line after a nerve wracking battle for the win at Indianapolis Motor Speedway.
(photo by: Streeter Lecka/Getty Images)

became its own distraction, its own impediment to fulfilling that dream. Reporters covering the NASCAR race at the Brickyard, especially those based in the Indianapolis area, naturally focus on Stewart and his chances each year. And since he'd never won there, the stories most always focused on his frustrations. The meltdown there in 2002 was the most obvious sign of just how deep

Stewart's misfortunes at Indy had drilled into his psyche, and the only thing that would change the focus would be success.

With the No. 20 team on the kind of roll it had been on leading into the 2005 Allstate 500, the attention was ramped up even higher. This, it seemed, could be the year.

Stewart had tested at the Indianapolis Motor Speedway and dealt

Photographers and media surround Stewart at the start/finish line of Indianapolis Motor Speedway. *(photo by: Streeter Lecka/Getty Images)*

with the first wave of questions. On the Tuesday before the race, he was the featured guest on a weekly NASCAR teleconference with reporters and talked even more.

"Any kid who grew up in Indiana knows what Indianapolis Motor Speedway means," Stewart said. "Obviously, we're talking about a different style of car with the Cup cars versus the Indy cars. But it's definitely my biggest race of the year. It always has been and probably always will be.

"At the same time, we have to treat it like another race and go through the motions just like another race and not let yourself get too consumed with the emotion of where we're at and what we're doing there. It's just a matter of going out and doing the work and hopefully being able to get there at the end of the day and kiss the bricks."

For the most part, Zipadelli said, the approach to that week was the same one that had seemed to be working so well in the previous weeks.

"Tony is having fun this year," Zipadelli said. "It's not that we haven't in the past. It's just a little bit different. He shows up at the race track really focused on winning and learning to control some of the things that used to aggravate him or be a distraction to him. ...We're just going to try to make light of the weekend and have fun and do the best we can. Hopefully I can tell him what we need to try to put ourselves in position to win and that's all you can ask."

Because Stewart's move back to Columbus had become so much a part of the season's emerging story about his success, the Thursday of The Allstate 400 week turned into media day in that town just 40 miles or so down the road. NASCAR beat writers from all over the country kept tripping over each other at the various places Stewart had talked about in his hometown. Bob Franke's Dairy Queen at Third and Lafayette, in fact, had reporters in and out pretty much all day.

Stewart has bought a large plot of land just west of town and plans to build a house there someday. For now, though, he seems perfectly happy in the house he lived in as a kid. He's put the bedroom he slept in back just like it was. He and his father, Nelson, are also going to redo the garage back to how it was when they worked there together on Tony's go-karts.

His high school, Columbus North, is only a couple of blocks away. In its 1988 yearbook Stewart, in his junior year, can be seen wearing a backward ball cap in a civics club photo.

About a month after he'd moved back home in 2004, a storm dumped two feet of snow on central Indiana. At 2:30 a.m. on Dec. 23, Nathan Nehrt's car got stuck as he tried to get home from work. Nehrt trudged home in the snow, but help soon came.

"NASCAR driver Tony Stewart and his friend Gary Pigg literally followed my footprints from my car to my house to offer their help," Nehrt wrote in a letter to the local newspaper. Stewart and Pigg used Stewart's pickup truck to tow Nehrt's car to his house. Before he got stuck, Nehrt had seen the same truck helping another stranded car at a local shopping center.

"When I asked them why they were going around helping everyone out, they said they were 'just having some fun,'" Nehrt wrote. "At a time when so many stories are focused on negative aspects of professional sports, it is nice to know there are still a few good guys."

Comparing what the folks in Columbus said about Stewart to the reputation that had been following him throughout his career in racing, it seemed there were almost two completely different Tony Stewarts.

"That's exactly right," Stewart said. "That's what the people in Columbus have found out. They realize I do what I do on the weekends. That's my job. But at home, I'm just another one of the guys.

"It's just a situation where you've got to stop and hit the reset button once in a while. Being around the stock car community seven days a week takes it's toll on you. The hard thing—especially living in Charlotte—is that I didn't have any friends there when I moved there. All the friends I had were on race teams and they worked during the day. ...There were a lot of times during the day that you were kind of bored and didn't know what to do and didn't have anybody to do anything with.

"I've got plenty of projects with my race teams around home to mess with and stuff to do with my property there. It gives me more opportunity to refresh myself to where when I do show up on a Cup weekend, I don't feel like I've been consumed with it for the four or five days before that when I wasn't at the track.

"All my friends are excited that I'm back home. They were all as sad about me moving to Charlotte as I was—even though I knew it was what I needed to do at the time. They understood that. You never want one of your friends to leave town. But they're all excited I'm back.

"The community itself has been awesome. I've joined the Moose Lodge and Eagles Lodge just to be a part of the community a little more. Through the winter was pretty busy and hectic. We typically would just stay away from the public. We'd just stay at home a lot and hang out with our friends. But I made the decision that when I moved home, I needed to be out more and let everybody see me and get used to me being there. As time goes on and everybody gets more accustomed to seeing me and people don't freak out when they see us and get that excited.

"I'm just another member of the community to most of them now. That's the way I want it. I don't want to be treated any different than anybody else. If you didn't know what I looked like, you wouldn't be able to pick me out of a crowd. The nice thing is that the community has welcomed me with open arms."

Practice was scheduled to begin Friday at Indianapolis Motor Speedway, but rain revamped the schedule. The practices were pushed back to Saturday morning, with qualifying moved to that afternoon. After the qualifying, cars would be impounded and would have to start in the same condition in which they ran in the time trials.

Elliott Sadler won the pole with a lap of 184.116 mph. Stewart, who said his car was little tight in the third turn, managed only 181.334 mph on his lap and that left him 22nd on the starting grid.

Stewart went to Indianapolis Raceway Park that night to compete in the NASCAR Busch Series race there. He would say later that helped him a lot. "There was a rain delay and it got over late," Stewart said. "So I got back late and didn't get into bed (at his motor coach at

(photo by: Worth Canoy/Icon SMI)

the track) till 1 and I slept till 9:30. I slept like a rock, like a baby. And when I woke up, I wasn't awake so long hearing all the music and seeing all the people coming in, I didn't get as worked up as I normally do."

Stewart had been at Indy for five Indianapolis 500 race days, including twice in "double duty" efforts after moving to NASCAR in which he drove in the 500 and NASCAR's Coca-Cola 600 at Charlotte's Lowe's Motor Speedway on the same day. He'd also raced in six Cup races at the track. And he'd never finished better than fifth.

Nelson Stewart, the father who'd helped Tony get started racing go-karts but who also had gone through some rocky times in their relationship when he and Tony's mother got a divorce, had once again become an important part of Stewart's life. He was there at Indy, sitting with dozens of other family members and friends in a suite above Turn 2 that Stewart has at IMS.

Nelson had watched as Stewart climbed the fences after the wins at Daytona and New Hampshire and felt he understood what his son was trying to do. "I think he's trying to make peace with himself and the fans," Nelson said. "Climbing the fence is one of those things where he can do it on his terms. He's bonding with the fans on his terms

(photo by: Rusty Jarrett/Getty Images)

instead of theirs. And he's comfortable with that."

By the halfway point of the race, Stewart had worked his way into the top five. On lap 100, he passed Brian Vickers to take the lead and pulled away to a lead of nearly four seconds.

A few laps later, Stewart noticed his father standing at the rail at the front of the Turn 2 suite.

"It's unbelievable that you can run as fast as you can in a race car and you can see things and pick up emotion," Stewart said. "To see the emotion on his face and to see how excited he was with his hands and fists in the air, I mean, that's when I got tears in my eyes. But I said, 'Hey, I've been in this position before.' Two laps later the tears went away, and it was back to business. Every year that I got the lead, I've got to see him do that. Today I thought, 'Man, I just want to finish it off one time.'

"I slipped once going through Turn 2. I came back around on the next lap and he's got his headset off and he's pointing to his head just like he did when I was 8 years old racing go-karts, saying 'use your head!' I'm sitting there thinking, 'Dad, I got here for a reason, because I know what I am doing. Just let me do my job.'"

And there was plenty more work to do. On lap 116, Stewart's Joe Gibbs Racing teammate Bobby Labonte lost a right-front tire to bring out a yellow flag. Stewart came in for four tires and fuel that maybe, with a few more caution laps

would be enough for him to go the rest of the way without stopping again.

But after the restart, another driver with Midwestern roots and a passion to win at Indianapolis tried to spoil Stewart's dream. Kasey Kahne, with whom Stewart had dueled so fiercely at Richmond earlier in the year, was coming hard in his No. 9 Dodge. On lap 134, Kahne passed Stewart to take over the lead. Stewart gave determined chase, but had it not been for a caution for Jimmie Johnson's wreck on lap 145 Stewart might never have had the chance to catch up.

Stewart wanted to come in for tires, but Zipadelli wanted him to stay on the track and maintain his position. For several seconds, they debated their strategy back and forth.

"I'm too nervous to make the call," Stewart said finally.

"Stay out," Zipadelli said.

"We aren't done yet," Stewart told Zipadelli. "I've come too far to give up now. I want this more than I want anything."

Zipadelli answered, "I know."

As the leaders came to the restart on lap 150 in the 160-lap race, Stewart marshaled his desire and talent toward the task at hand. "I am just trying to pull something out of my bag of tricks here to see what I have left," Stewart said.

Stewart's winning move wasn't terribly tricky. He laid back a bit on the restart and then dove hard into Turn 1, edging himself underneath Kahne and sliding into the lead. Kahne fought back

(photo by: Rusty Jarrett/Getty Images)

as hard as Stewart had earlier, shadowing Stewart down the straightaways.

With three laps to go, Stewart was eight-tenths of a second ahead. But did he have the fuel, or would cruel fate intervene and break Stewart's heart at Indianapolis one more time?

"Four more corners," Stewart's spotter said as the No. 20 came off Turn 4 and saw the white flag.

The massive crowd in Indy's grandstands rose to its feet. There would be no heartbreak this time. Only elation.

"YES!" Stewart yelled after taking the checkered flag. "I love you guys, you've helped me live my lifelong dream today."

The catchfence at Indianapolis Motor Speedway is particularly high, with a particularly tough curve to get over or around near the top. Stewart's crew, however, was ready—they had a ladder that they brought onto the track and told their driver they'd climb it with him.

"I'm too tired to get to the top," he said over his radio. Besides, he had other plans. He took the No. 20 on a long, slow lap around the track in the reverse direction, waving to the crowd and drinking in the satisfaction of a dream accomplished. When he got to the Turn 2, where his family and friends had been watching from his suite, Stewart stopped the car and got out.

Stewart climbed atop the wall, slapped a high-five through the fence with one fan, and popped open a cold soda he'd been handed by his crew back over on the frontstretch.

"TO-NY! TO-NY! TO-NY!" the crowd yelled as he toasted his family in the suite and his friends—all of them, symbolically,—who'd been there to witness him do the one thing he'd always most wanted to do.

When he made it back around after the most satisfying lap he'd ever made at the historic Indy track, Stewart did get up on the fence in the frontstretch for just a moment. But he came back down and laid down on the wall.

"I feel like crap right now," he said to an NBC reporter, "but in five minutes I am going to feel real good."

There's absolutely no way it took that long.

(photo by: Streeter Lecka/Getty Images)

2005 Nextel Cup Champion

TONY STEWART

(photo by: Worth Canoy/Icon SMI)

Stewart's postrace celebration with his team, his crew and his fans who were there that day stretched on and on. Through all the trophy presentations, the kissing of the bricks, the hugs and handshakes from what must have been the entire population of Columbus, Stewart was smiling the kind of smile that only comes from ultimate satisfaction.

"Today," he'd say later, "has been my entire life."

More than two hours after the race, Stewart made it to the media center to talk at length about his victory. His family and friends had already decided when and where the party would be, quickly arranging for a room at a downtown hotel. They'd have to wait a while for the guest of honor, though.

"This is one of those days that I don't want it to end," Stewart said. "I don't want to see the sun set. If I could make this day longer, I'd do it in a heartbeat

(photo by: Worth Canoy/Icon SMI)

The crowd was on its feet as Stewart crossed the finish line.
(photo by: Worth Canoy/Icon SMI)

because this is probably—well, it's definitely the greatest day of my life up to this point professionally, personally. I mean, I couldn't ask for more. I mean, I don't even know what to say about it. I know part of it hasn't sunk in yet.

"Since I was a little kid, I've always wanted to just compete at the Brickyard. Then when I realized that, I was like, we ran so well and missed, it was like, I know I can win at the Brickyard one day. And so finally today was that day."

Down in Columbus, as soon as the race ended people started coming by the Dairy Queen for the town's unofficial celebration. Bob Franke's daughter, Julie, said they gave away nearly 1,000 "Tony shakes."

Back up in Indianapolis, Stewart was still reminiscing. He was asked what he remembered about the first time he'd ever come to Indianapolis for the 500-miler in May.

"One of them I remember I came here with my father," he said. "I don't even remember why we were in this bus, but we were in some bus that had a luggage rack in the top of it. You had to get up at 'oh-dark-thirty' to get on the bus to ride up here for race day. They threw me up in the luggage rack. Somebody had a pillow. Everybody started throwing their jackets

on top of me to keep me warm. Then the ride home wasn't near as cool because everybody was drunk on the bus except for my dad and I. And everybody was trying to give me beer. I was probably 5 years old."

And now here he was, on what he'd already called the greatest day of his life, drinking it all in.

Oh, by the way, he was also now the NASCAR Nextel Cup points leader.

Winner
July 17, 2005

NASCAR
NEXTEL
CUP SERIES

NEW
ENGLAND
300
NEW HAMPSHIRE
INTERNATIONAL SPEEDWAY

NEW HAMPSHIRE
INTERNATIONAL SPEEDWAY

(photo by: Worth Canoy/Icon SMI)

CHAPTER **6**

If the drivers who all now found themselves behind Stewart in the standings were looking for a post-Indianapolis letdown, they were sadly disappointed.

Stewart won the pole for the season's second road-course race at Watkins Glen, N.Y., then led 83 of 92 laps to win for the second straight week and for the fifth time in seven races.

"We had a pretty flawless day," Stewart said. "I've had zones...when I was in midgets and sprint cars where I could go week in and week out and not fall out of the top three. But to win five of the past seven and be in the top seven for the past eight weeks is a pretty good record."

Pretty good? Stewart's run had sent people scurrying to the record books to figure out when anyone had been that hot. Late in the 1998 season, on his way to a championship and a modern-era record 13 victories that year, Gordon won four

straight and seven of nine races over one stretch.

Four races remained until the cutoff to the Chase, and Stewart and his team were cruising toward a spot in the 10-driver contest for the championship. As other teams scrambled to make the cut, the No. 20 team kept putting up solid runs. A fifth at Michigan, eighth at Bristol, fifth at California and, finally, a seventh at Richmond that left Stewart 185 points clear of Biffle atop the standings. But under the new championship format, Stewart saw 180 of those disappear overnight. As the 10 contenders—Stewart, Biffle, Rusty Wallace, Johnson, defending champion Kurt Busch, Mark Martin, Jeremy Mayfield, Carl Edwards, Matt Kenseth and Ryan Newman—went to New Hampshire for the season's second race there, Stewart's lead was just five points over Biffle and 45 over 10th-place Newman.

Stewart celebrates as he made a sweep of the NASCAR Nextel Cup road course races in 2005. *(photo by: Brian Cleary/Icon SMI)*

(photo by: Brian Cleary/Icon SMI)

2005 Nextel Cup Champion

The field for the Chase for the Nextel Cup was set for 2005. Back row l-r: Greg Biffle, Jimmie Johnson, Rusty Wallace, Carl Edwards, Jeremy Mayfield and Tony Stewart. Front row l-r: Matt Kenseth, Mark Martin, Kurt Busch and Ryan Newman.
(photo by: Worth Canoy/Icon SMI)

A dozen straight finishes of eighth or better had carried Stewart through the summer, but they really no longer did him a whole lot of good. In the Chase for the Nextel Cup, it's performance in the final 10 races that determines the winner. At no point, however, did Stewart seem all that worried.

"We're in a better position and better mode than we were then," he said when

asked to compare 2005 to the first time he'd won the title. "Even in 2002 when we won I was running us all through some turmoil at the same time....This year we're probably getting along as good if not better than we were in 1999 when we didn't have a care in the world. At that time there wasn't any pressure on us, we were just out there having fun as a young race team and I think we've been able to,

TONY STEWART

over the off-season, kind of recapture that.

"If we have a bad day, it's a bad day. It seems like the worst thing that can happen is to let it get to you and get you down and that's something that Zippy has worked really hard on with all the guys and me as well. Now the morale of the team is up even when we have a bad day. It doesn't mean we accept losing better, but we don't let it dictate the rest of our week or the following weeks after that. We just shrug it off and say, 'OK, now we have to work on next week and try to find something to make us better than the week before.'

"I just feel like we have a really strong group of guys. We've had the same core group of people for so long, I mean, it's hard to have a combination like that. There's not very many teams out there that are still like that. I'm really proud of the group of people that Zippy's assembled and there's always new people getting added to it but you don't see a lot of people going away from us and that's something I think is making us a stronger team every year."

But it was more than having team unity that marked the difference in Stewart. He'd seemed to find his own kind of peace. He could still needle one of his team members or a garage-area regular with great skill, and he still had his somewhat off-center sense of humor.

"One of the things we always say is it's all in good fun until somebody gets

hurt," Stewart said. "And then, it's hilarious."

There's a line in the great old country song "Mamas Don't Let Your Babies Grow Up to be Cowboys," that goes like this: "Them that don't know him won't like him and them that do sometimes won't know how to take him." Stewart's still got a little bit of that in him.

"At the end of the day, I've got to go drive race cars and when I go home I don't worry about whether I was misunderstood or not anymore," he said. "I've just simplified everything. I quit worrying about stuff like that. "

I could do an interview with 10 people and I could give the same quote. If nine of them took it one way and one person takes it a different way, I can't control that. Whether I feel like I'm misinterpreted or whatever, it doesn't really matter.

"As long as I'm happy when I go home and the people I'm around are happy and don't have a problem with what I'm doing, in all reality I shouldn't worry about it. You can't please everybody 100 percent of the time anyway and to be honest, it's just made everything a lot easier when I finally just quit worrying about it. It seems like I've gotten less stressed out about it and been less edgy because of it.

"The single biggest thing that drives me nuts is having to answer questions about things that happened a year ago or two or three or four years ago. There's nothing I can do about those previous years. There is nothing I can do to erase it. All I can do is control what happens from this moment forward. ...I've had a better year this year. I haven't annoyed everybody. I've tried to be a little better with the photographers and media and fans. Everybody has kind of noticed that. Still, every week somebody's got something in there about terrible Tony and this or that. Now what am I doing wrong? That's the stuff that gets annoying."

The Chase began at New Hampshire, where Stewart's Chevrolet had been so dominant in July. He led 173 more laps in the September race, but got his car dinged in a bump with Dale Earnhardt Jr. and wound up losing a late-race duel with Newman and wound up second.

"That was awesome short-track racing right there," Stewart said. "The fans got their money's worth today. That's the way the race to the Chase should start, just like that. It should be between three of the top guys in the series who are racing for the championship. Ryan did an awesome job. We just couldn't hold him off."

Stewart had led the points standings since Indianapolis, but he fell to fifth after a puzzling second Chase race at Dover, Del. Stewart and Zipadelli just couldn't get a handle on their car and he finished 18th.

"Nobody saw this coming for sure," Stewart said. "I don't know why it was so bad today, but I thank all these guys on this Home Depot team. None of us gave

up all day. I'm just proud of them. It was a lot better car at the end than from where we started."

Stewart was tied with Biffle, 23 points back in the standings, heading to Talladega. The UAW-Ford 500 figured to be one of the most important races in the Chase, since the 2.66-mile track is known as a place where just about anything can happen. And, indeed, trouble started early for several Chase contenders. Johnson finished 31st after getting a piece of both of the day's big wrecks. Martin, Wallace and Biffle took hits, too, finishing 41st, 25th and 27th, respectively.

Stewart, meanwhile, led 65 laps in another strong restrictor-plate run. He managed that despite having to spend time on pit road during the race with his hood up and his team trying to cool down an engine that was running hot.

"I looked at the water gauge and it was about 265 (degrees)...and it kept climbing to 275 and we had the fan on and everything," Stewart said. "I couldn't do anything else inside the car. ...We could never really get a handle on it.

"I kept trying to duck out and get some fresh air to it but it never brought it down like it typically does in practice. But we just kept coming in and kept peeling a strip of tape off at a time. We finally ended up peeling all the tape off the car. I'm sure that slowed it down a little bit but at the same time at least we got the heat issue under control."

At the end of the race, which featured a green-white-checkered finish, Stewart

Tony credits Zippy with having held the team together and keeping morale high when things have not gone their way. *(photo by: Jerome Davis/Icon SMI)*

drove to the inside of Kenseth's Ford as he tried to get the lead back. Dale Jarrett, who'd helped push Stewart by Newman's car, had moved to the outside, getting a push from Carl Edwards. On the final lap, Jarrett kept getting that push from behind and went all the way to the lead and the victory. Stewart finished second for the fifth time in his career at Talladega without a win. But with the problems suffered by others in the Chase, he did move back into the lead in the standings, just four points ahead of Newman.

Stewart finished fourth at Kansas, yet another solid run, in a race that Martin won. Then came the season's second visit to Charlotte's Lowe's Motor Speedway and a UAW-GM 500 that didn't turn out the way anyone expected.

At the Coca-Cola 600 in May, the race at the 1.5-mile Charlotte track had been interrupted by 22 yellow flags—more than any race at any track in the history of NASCAR's top series. Much of the track's surface had been ground to smooth out bumps that had developed since its last repaving, and that process got at least part of the blame for all of those wrecks. For the fall race, more of the track had been ground and Goodyear had brought back the same tire. Because the track was so smooth, tires did not wear out during

Tony Stewart leads the way early in the Sylvania 300 at New Hampshire International Speedway.
(photo by: Worth Canoy/Icon SMI)

TONY STEWART

the race. Instead, the traction that was maintained led to a build-up in heat in the tires, and that led to a rash of tire failures.

Stewart led 61 laps in the UAW-GM 500, but on lap 216 he had a tire blow out and that sent his No. 20 Chevrolet into the wall. His crew swept into action and made repairs as well and as quickly as they could, and with others falling out of the race too the toll that race took on his title hopes wasn't as bad as it might have

been. Stewart finished 25th and held the points lead, but only by the slimmest possible margin. He'd led by 75 points when the race began, but when Johnson won the race he made up all of that deficit. They were tied at 5,777 points, but since Stewart had won five races to four for Johnson, Stewart was still the leader based on the first tiebreaker.

"We did the best with what we had," Stewart said. "We had the fastest car. ...It

Even with blistering fast pit stops, several of the "Chasers" were unable to make much headway at Lowes Motor Speedway in October, as tire problems were the rule of the day. (photo by: Erik Perel/Icon SMI)

was just a weird night. This is just what we had to deal with. We'll take our lumps and we'll go on from here.

"We were pulling away in the points tonight. We should have been 100 points ahead (but) instead I'm tied for the lead. ...But you know what, in this series, nothing surprises me anymore. I thought I'd seen all the craziest things I think I could see in this sport. Who knows what's going to happen?"

What happened next, in the Subway 500 at Martinsville Speedway, was that after a weekend in which the media tried to draw Johnson into a controversy over something that Johnson's crew chief, Chad Knaus, supposedly said over his team's radio during a practice on Saturday.

"It wasn't Jimmie," Stewart said. "It was, of all people, his crew chief trying to play games like we used to do in the seventh grade."

Johnson said there was no menace intended. "Stuff like that gets said on the radio all the time," he said. "It's your guys' job to twist it and turn it and find something to write about and have fun with it."

The Subway 500 was fun to watch, too. Stewart led 283 of the first 343 laps

Stewart leads his teammate, Bobby Labonte, around Lowes Motor Speedway. Towards the end of 2005 it was announced that Labonte will go to Petty Enterprises in 2006 and J.J. Yeley will drive the No. 18 for Joe Gibbs Racing. *(photo by: Worth Canoy/Icon SMI)*

but when pit strategy turned track position around Jeff Gordon emerged with the lead and Stewart found himself battling with Johnson for position and, along with it, the top spot in the Chase. Stewart was behind both Gordon and Johnson on a restart on lap 436 and had to battle past Biffle, as Biffle tried to keep from being lapped, before getting into position to challenge Johnson for second. Stewart got the spot with a hello-and-goodbye bump, but couldn't catch Gordon and had to settle for his sixth runner-up finish of the year.

"I just got hit from behind," Johnson said. "He got in there far enough to knock me out of the way. If I could have gotten back to him, I would have returned the favor."

Johnson finished third, but because he didn't lead a lap and because Stewart led the most laps, Stewart left the Virginia track with a 15-point lead in the standings.

Stewart gained more ground with a ninth-place finish at Atlanta as Johnson finished 16th, then finished sixth to Johnson's fifth at Texas. Carl Edwards won the Atlanta and Texas races to move into third in the standings, 77 points behind Stewart and 39 behind Johnson. Stewart went to Phoenix determined to

Tony and eventual winner Dale Jarrett bring the field around at Talladega International Speedway.
(photo by: Matthew Stockman/Getty Images)

NASCAR action in the desert during the Checker Auto Parts 500 at Phoenix International Raceway in Phoenix, Ariz. *(photo by: Brian Cleary/Icon SMI)*

keep right on doing what he'd been doing to put himself in position to win a second championship.

"It really is going to boil down to something as simple as going out and doing the same things the same way we did to get ourselves in the lead," Stewart said. "We're not watching where everybody else is. ...We don't have to make something happen. Everybody else has to make something happen.

"We're not controlling the whole Chase. But we are controlling the side of it that we can, and that's with our car. That's what made it so easy for us. You look at the other teams and they're all focusing on what we're doing. We like that. We want them to do that. That lets us focus on what we're doing and not what they're doing."

In the Checker Auto Parts 500, Stewart did exactly what he'd been doing since Michigan in June. He finished fourth in a race won by Kyle Busch, two positions ahead of Edwards and three ahead of Johnson. It gave Stewart a 52-point lead over Johnson and an 87-point edge on Edwards going into the final race of the season at Homestead-Miami Speedway.

Going into the finale, Stewart needed to finish ninth or better to clinch the championship no matter where anybody else finished. Given that he'd finished ninth or better in 19 of his previous 21 races at that track, all he needed was more of the same.

Tony wasn't able to take home a win at the Subway 500, but did what he had to do to position himself back atop the Nextel Cup standings.
(photo by: Worth Canoy/Icon SMI)

(photo by: John Pyle/Icon SMI)

CHAPTER 7

NASCAR is trying to build the final week of its season into a "championship week" that at least partly rivals the build-up to the Super Bowl or the NCAA Final Four.

The final races in all three NASCAR national series—Nextel Cup, Busch and CraftsmanTrucks—are now held each year at the Homestead-Miami Speedway about 30 miles south of Miami. In 2005, all three series brought their championship battles to these final races with the titles still to be determined.

Veteran Ted Musgrave, at age 49, would wrap up his first title in the NASCAR Craftsman Truck Series in a race delayed by rain from Friday night until Saturday morning. Later that day, Martin Truex Jr. would also wrap up a title, his second straight, in the NASCAR Busch Series. But the main event was the

Ford 400, the NASCAR Nextel Cup finale scheduled for late Sunday afternoon which, since the 2004 season has ended into the evening hours under the lights.

The hype began on Thursday at a hotel near the Miami airport that NASCAR had designated as the media's headquarters. The four drivers still mathematically in the title picture gathered to talk about their seasons and the weekend ahead. As Tony Stewart, Jimmie Johnson, Carl Edwards and Greg Biffle talked that day, though, it was clear that there would be no trash-talking "sound byte" coming from this media day—as there sometimes is before championship events in other sports. This, frankly, was a mutual admiration society meeting.

"Even though the goal is fighting hard against each other on the race track, at

Stewart and his team celebrate after capturing the 2005 NASCAR Nextel Cup Championship. *(photo by: Worth Canoy/Icon SMI)*

the end of the day, we are all friends and we all get along with each other and we all enjoy what we're doing," Stewart said. "That's probably one of the gratifications of winning a championship, is you're competing against guys that you have respect for and that you like and that you can get along and have fun with."

Biffle was the long shot in the group, coming into the last race fourth in the standings and 102 points behind Stewart.

"I know how hard I've worked to be here," Biffle said. "I know how much I've done and you have so much respect for the other guys...because you know what they had to do."

With all three series sharing track time on Friday, touch-and-go weather shuffled the schedule around somewhat. By the time the Nextel Cup cars got on the track for their final practice before qualifying scheduled for early Saturday

The No. 20 team brings the Home Depot Chevrolet back to the garage after practice.
(photo by: Bob Leverone/TSN/ZUMA Press/Icon SMI)

afternoon, it was already dark and the lights were on.

Stewart's car had been so-so on the speed charts in the first session a couple of hours earlier. But early in that second practice he spun out while running a lap. Stewart managed to keep the car from hitting the wall, and there was no evidence that anything on the car had been significantly damaged. Crew chief Greg Zipadelli and his crew would go over it carefully, checking to see if the spin might have damaged something hidden down in the engine, but came away satisfied that the car and the motor would be good to go. Still, the spin was unnerving. Stewart said without a clear idea of what had caused it; the spin had made him a little gun-shy for the rest of weekend.

"It kind of got us, I'm not going to say in thrash mode, but it broke my confidence not knowing why I spun," he would say later. "I knew I was a little bit free but I didn't think I was going to lose a car like that."

Zipadelli put a very conservative set-up under the car for qualifying. Since the Ford 400 would be an impound race, Stewart would have to start his No. 20 Chevrolet the way he ran it on his qualifying lap. Not wanting to be too loose when the race began the next day,

Stewart qualified only 20th best. That still left him ahead of Johnson, who'd start 32nd, but behind Edwards, who won the pole, and Biffle, who was seventh fastest.

There were rain showers in the forecast for race day, and there were a few sprinkles a couple of hours before the 4 p.m. start. But the weather held off and the race began on time. There were just 267 laps between Stewart and his second title.

Stewart moved up from 20th to well inside the top 15 in the early laps. Johnson got an early scare when he barely dodged Scott Wimmer's spinning car, and not too long after that Stewart had an all-too-close view of a Kyle Busch spin. Edwards, meanwhile, led the first lap to get five bonus points, and then dropped back behind Ryan Newman before resurging into the lead.

Just after the race moved past its first 100 laps, there were significant developments. Stewart was holding his own around the 10th position, but Johnson's No. 48 Chevrolet started to loose ground. He thought he might have a tire going down, but if he pitted for that and there was no problem he might be giving away his last shot at winning the title. Johnson tried to hold on until a caution flag came out, but on lap 125 he brought the caution out himself when a right-rear tire went down and sent Johnson into the wall. His day was done. He'd finish 40th and, by day's end, drop all the way from second to fifth in the final standings.

Stewart had a little more room to work with. He'd come into the last race needing to finish ninth to eliminate everyone from contention. Johnson, however, had eliminated himself with his problems and now it was Edwards who

was the closest rival. Stewart now needed only to run 20th to beat Edwards—and Biffle, who'd started the day even further back.

Stewart's car was getting tight as it continued each run, meaning it was hard to turn. He fell back as far as 17th at one point—leaving not much room for error with Edwards leading the race and putting himself in position to score the maximum points by leading the most laps, too.

The No. 20 team performs another flawless pitstop during the Ford 400 at Homestead-Miami Speedway. (*photo by: Worth Canoy/Icon SMI*)

As his boss Jeff Gordon goes by him, Jimmie Johnson has a tire go down which ends his chances at the championship.
(photo by: Worth Canoy/Icon SMI)

"We started a little bit more conservative than we needed to, and were probably that way for the first couple of adjustments," Zipadelli said. "We had gotten a lot better at the end, but at that point we had given up so much track position. But, it was all about coming in here and doing what we needed to do. I hate to say, but we had to play it safe. We didn't need to take any chances in any areas."

It helped Stewart's cause that Edwards, who would lead the most laps—94—by the checkered flag, had lost the lead to Casey Mears as the race moved into its final 50 laps. Mears seemed to be on the way to his first career win until a late caution. Stewart tried to stay out to

TONY STEWART

lead a lap and get five more points, but Dave Blaney had the same idea and thwarted the plan. Stewart was running 15th, the last car on the lead lap, so the move cost him nothing. He merely stopped a lap later and got fresh tires for what would be an 11-lap run to the checkered flag.

Edwards took four tires, but just about everyone else took two. Edwards was 10th on the restart and needed to make up ground in a hurry. Biffle was fourth when the green flew, and he quickly got up to the front while his tires were still fresh. He made a three-wide pass on Blaney and Mark Martin and spent the final three laps fending off Martin, ultimately winning the race by less than half of a car-length.

Edwards made it back to fourth place. He and Biffle wound up with the same number of points, 6,498, but Biffle won six races to Edwards' four, giving Biffle the tiebreaker. But that tie being broken was for second place. Stewart had finished 15th, but he'd also gotten to the end of the season with 35 more points than Biffle and Edwards. The championship was his, making Stewart

"Smoke" celebrates with a burnout and a victory lap after coming out on top in the 2005 Chase for the Nextel Cup.
(photo by: Brian Cleary/Icon SMI)

the 14th driver to win more than one title in NASCAR's top series.

"Are you going to climb the fence?" a crewman asked Stewart as he came around to start his championship celebration.

"No," Stewart said. "I just want to get back over there and celebrate with you guys."

Later on, Stewart and the crew did go up on the frontstretch fence after the fans chanted a request that they do so. But this time, the team came first. The hard lessons from the past had been learned.

"Even when we weren't running good, we were having fun," Stewart said. "We got back to why we started racing in the first place and that's because we love being a part of race teams and we love racing and we love competing. That attitude carried us through the slow times and when the good times happened, it just made it that much better for us. We were a stronger team this year than the entire time I've been with Joe Gibbs Racing.

"Nobody is ever going to accuse me of being smarter. And I'm not going to say

(photo by: Brian Cleary/Icon SMI)

2005 Nextel Cup Champion

Stewart climbs the fence one last time in the 2005 Nextel Cup season.
(photo by: Jason Arnold/Icon SMI)

I'm a better driver. I think that we're just a better team. Our organization has grown and grown stronger. You know, I feel I'm just a piece of the puzzle. I feel we all complement each other well.

"The greatest strength of Joe Gibbs has been assembling the right people to do the right jobs. And the great thing with that is that when we were behind early in the season, we didn't know which area was going to get us caught up. So, the motor department dug in, the fab shop dug in. Zippy and the guys on the pit stops dug in. I dug in. We all tried to get that extra half percent or percent that we all thought we needed.

"I'm just a piece of the puzzle. I'm not the guy that won us this championship. This race team won us this championship."

After the finale, Mark Martin heaped praise on the champion. "Tony Stewart, in my eyes, is the greatest race car driver I've watched drive in this era," Martin said. "A.J. Foyt might have been that when I was a little boy, but Tony Stewart is my driving hero."

On the day in August when Stewart won at Indianapolis, he'd called that the greatest day of his life. That Sunday at Homestead, though, was a pretty good

(photo by: Harold Hinson/TSN/ Zuma Press/Icon SMI)

2005 Nextel Cup Champion

day, too. Stewart had won the championship, as he put it, "the right way."

How much more can he accomplish?

"When it's all said and done and no matter when I quit, whether it is 20 years or five years or whenever it is, what is going to be left from all this is the relationships that were built along the way," Stewart said. "I can't look into the future. I don't know what the rest of my life is going to be like. I don't know how long I'm going to race. I've never even thought of retiring. But...I've (already) had a great life up to this point. I couldn't have asked for more.

"I feel like I'm a very, very, very fortunate person, not only on the personal side of my life to have friends that wouldn't care if I drove another lap in a race car the rest of my life, but to have the professional life that I have, too. ...No matter how long I race or don't race, the goals and everything that happens from here are just icing on the cake. I think I've done more at this point in my life than a lot of the guys have that have been fortunate enough to do this and I've been very lucky to be able to do the things we've done."

(photo by: Bob Leverone/TSN/
Zuma Press/Icon SMI)